P9-EMN-516

CREATIVE TRAINING TOOLS

101

Easy-to Use Ideas

for Increasing

Trainee

Participation

■ ■ ■

By Bob Pike with Julie Tilka

Lakewood Publications
A Maclean Hunter Company

Quantity Sales

Most Lakewood books are available at special quantity discounts when purchased in bulk by companies, organizations and special-interest groups. Custom imprinting or excerpting can also be done to fit special needs. For details contact Lakewood Books.

■ ■ ■

LAKEWOOD BOOKS
50 South Ninth Street
Minneapolis, MN 55402
(800) 707-7769 or (612) 333-0471
FAX (612) 340-4819

Publisher: Philip G. Jones
Editors: Bob Pike with Julie Tilka
Production Editor: Julie Tilka
Production: Carol Swanson and Pat Grawert
Cover Designer: Barb Betz, Betz Design

10 9 8 7 6 5 4 3 2 1

Lakewood Publications, Inc. publishes *TRAINING Magazine; Training Directors' Forum Newsletter; Creative Training Techniques Newsletter; Technology For Learning Newsletter; Potentials In Marketing* Magazine, *Presentations* Magazine; and other business periodicals, books, research and conferences.

Bob Pike, Creative Training Techniques International, 7620 W. 78th St., Edina, MN 55439, (612) 829-1960, FAX (612) 829-0260.

ISBN 0-943210-69-0

Contents

Foreword

This book, *Creative Training Tools*, is one in a series drawn from the best content of *Creative Training Techniques Newsletter*. The newsletter was conceived in 1988 by editor and internationally known trainer Bob Pike to be a one-stop resource of practical "how-tos" for trainers. The idea was (and still is) to provide timely tips, techniques, and strategies that help trainers with the special tasks they perform daily.

When the newsletter began, it was largely fueled by Bob's 20 years of experience in the field and by the best ideas shared by the trainers (more than 50,000 in all) who had attended his Creative Training Techniques seminars. As the newsletter grew in popularity, it also began to draw on ideas submitted by its readers. Today, the newsletter continues to search out creative approaches from the more than 200 seminars Bob and the other Creative Training Techniques trainers conduct every year, and from the newsletter readers.

But no matter where the insights come from, the goal of the newsletter remains the same: To provide trainers a cafeteria of ideas they can quickly absorb, and then choose those that best suit their special needs.

This series of books represents the best ideas from *Creative Training Techniques Newsletter's* six years of publication. It is our hope we've created a valuable resource you'll come back to again and again to help address the unique challenges you face in your job every day.

Sincerely,
The Editors

Introduction

"If you tell me, I may listen. If you show me, I may understand. If you involve me, I will learn."

These ancient words of wisdom are the foundation on which the ideas and techniques presented in *Creative Training Tools* are built.

The soul of any successful session is involvement. People learn and remember by doing. This volume provides 101 simple, cost-effective ideas for enlivening your classroom — and getting participants to take an active role in learning.

The "tools" presented on these pages are as simple as goldfish, magnets, and old hats. But underlying that simplicity are valuable, practical lessons for building skills in the classroom that aid trainees when they return to the workplace.

Participants may be skeptical when you hand them a can of Play-Doh and ask them to create a sculpture that represents a learning point from your session. But when they begin molding it with their hands, they realize creativity is boundless — that it creates new, enjoyable ways to look at problems and situations.

Creative techniques boost not only learning, but bonding. A simple project done in the company of others creates intimacy and openness of a kind not easily created any other way. A completed piece of "art" that might seem like child's play in any other context becomes a tool for remembering people — as well as lessons.

New ideas from training peers — the kind this book presents — can help you avoid burnout and keep your sessions fresh. Putting a new twist on your 57th session of "Fundamentals of Supervision" makes *your* day a little more refreshing, and in turn, improves the quality of your presentation for your audience.

The classroom is a creative playground. The energy put into finding and implementing new participant-centered approaches to training pays off in increased energy and enjoyment in your training day. Have fun.

Bob Pike

Creative Training Tools

Sometimes participants need reminding of the sage advice to take their *work* seriously, but not *themselves*. The old saw has a new usefulness in these times of growing job stress created by downsizing and increased global competition.

At the end of a seminar, Cindy Rowan, founder of Career Investments in Newfoundland, NJ, asks participants to write their names and phone numbers on pieces of paper. She then asks them to jot down something that will remind them about keeping perspective and taking their senses of humor seriously — a word, phrase, or a punch line that'll make them laugh.

She then asks each to make a paper airplane from that sheet and on the count of three, toss them into the air. Everyone picks up an airplane and is told to call that person in a week, repeating what is written on the paper and immediately hanging up. Rowan suggests they call again in another week, repeat the word or punch line again and this time stay on the line, introducing themselves and having a chat.

1

Airplane activity reminds trainees to lighten up

2

Chaotic 'kazooing' helps break class into groups

Trainers often divide a class into small groups with some variation on the "find people who match you" exercise: Participants, for example, draw slips and make the sound of an animal drawn on their paper. The end goal is to unite with others like yourself.

Peggy Geib, a training coordinator at MetraTech, Oklahoma City, OK, energizes students with her own variation. She gives participants kazoos and asks them to select the name of a simple song — "Happy Birthday," "Yankee Doodle," "Mary Had a Little Lamb" — from a box. There are several slips showing each song title. The number of titles is equal to the number of small groups Geib wants to create.

Geib instructs attendees to play the song they've selected on their kazoos and to locate others playing the same tune. Less-outgoing folks are protected from being made overly uncomfortable, she says, because the cacophony makes telling one "musician" from another difficult for anyone not nearby.

Rosemary Bishop, a senior retail trainer at Hallmark Cards, Kansas City, MO, demonstrates the importance of teamwork by asking participants how many pennies they've handled in their lives. Many offer numbers in the millions.

She then divides the class into groups of three or four and instructs each group to make two circles on a sheet of paper, and — without looking at a coin — to draw the "head" of a penny in one and the "tail" side in the other. One person draws while the others offer tips.

The exercise teaches participants to appreciate the input of others in accomplishing tasks, and gives them a new appreciation for things one might normally take for granted.

3

It only takes a penny to show what teamwork can do

4

Pennies puzzler gets trainees to think creatively

To stress creativity and "thinking out of the box," Cindy Forbes, the assistant vice president of MBNA America in Newark, DE, gives each training participant 12 pennies and asks them to form a square with five pennies on each side. After giving trainees an appropriate amount of time to solve the puzzler, she explains the solution. When the solution is explained it helps participants realize their thinking was unnecessarily restrictive, she says.

Forbes uses this exercise to discuss the benefit of finding creative solutions to problems.

Pennies puzzler solution

Stack two pennies on top of each other for each of the four corners, then place one penny between each corner to form a square.

Often training participants are unaware when they're being negative, so Susan Berg, a training and education specialist at Kimball Office Furniture in Jasper, IN, developed a group technique that helps these trainees realize what they are saying and gives other class members a chance to help those people recognize the detrimental effect on the session.

The technique is called "Nerf the Negative." First, post a list of killer phrases such as, "It's been done," "We've tried it," or "It'll never work." Then, during the session, if anyone uses one of these phrases, anyone and everyone can bomb the negative person. All that's required is a supply of Nerfballs.

It's important, says Berg, to explain there are no wrong or dumb ideas at the beginning of the session. Any idea, no matter how unusual it may sound, is worthwhile. Only negative phrases are open game for a Nerfball barrage.

• Tina Johnson, a human resources manager at HS Healthcare Inc., Savoy, IL, adds to the idea by suggesting participants bomb the instructor if the instructor is guilty of talking down to or way above the participants with jargon not previously explained.

5

'Nerfing' negative trainees keeps focus on positive

6

Exercise's payoff is your trainees' undivided attention

Money talks — even if it is play money — in classes conducted by Deb Skow, a training instructor with the California Department of Motor Vehicles, Sacramento, CA. Skow uses the "payoff" technique to encourage trainees to use the course reference materials, participate in class, and remain attentive.

On the first day of a computer training class, for example, each trainee gets "funny money" consisting of 20 $1 bills. Skow displays a "Penalty Chart" that lists the various infractions and the cost of each, and a "Bonus Chart" that shows good practices that can earn trainees "money" (see accompanying charts on next page).

Then, throughout the training session, if a participant is asked a question, doesn't know the answer, and then fails to look it up, the first person to find the answer may collect the amount indicated on the Penalty Chart from the "offender." If a trainee is caught committing any offense listed, *one* other person may charge them the amount indicated for the offense. (The trainer has the final say in any dispute.)

All trainees can earn "Bonus bucks" by performing activities that are shown on the Bonus Chart.

On the last day of class, the trainee with the most funny money wins a prize.

Penalty Chart

Failing to look up an answer in:

Registration manual $1

Registration technical manual ... $2

Trainee's journal $2

Talking while trainer is explaining
   something $3

Keying before instructed
   to do so $3

Not pressing final "enter" $2

Failure to sign-off computer
   when leaving $3

Bonus Chart

A quiz score of:

80% - 89% $1

90% - 99% $2

Volunteering to go first $5

Sharing topic-related experiences
   with class $2

Any act that benefits the
   entire class .... $2-$5

7

Three-sided card provides instant interest assessment

To determine how she is keeping participants' interest during a training session, Erika Fleig, a training specialist for GE Capital in Jacksonville, FL, asks participants to fold a piece of heavy construction paper into thirds and stand the "tent card" on end (or on its side).

She then asks them to draw a happy face on one side, a sleepy face on another, and a confused face on a third side.

Throughout the course, Fleig asks participants to show the faces that reflect their interest in the material being covered. In addition, she says this allows those who are less comfortable speaking up in a group the opportunity to voice their opinions.

Depending on which face a trainee displays, the instructor can get an instant visual feedback during a learning unit.

Rather than lecturing on changes that have taken place in teaching over the past 20 years during teacher training, Cathy Duvall, an instructional specialist at the Fort Bend Independent School District, Sugar Land, TX, uses artifacts and equipment from then and now as discussion starters. She breaks the class into groups of three to six teachers and gives each a bag of old or new items to examine one by one.

Duvall then asks the groups to describe the classrooms where the items were originally used. She says describing a classroom of 20 years ago helps students see how much teaching has changed.

8

Look into past sets stage for new methods

The Old Paradigm
- Spelling book.
- Red checking pen.
- Fill-in-the-blank ditto sheets.
- Lesson plan book, detailed by time increments, page numbers, step-by-step routines.
- Chalk.
- Class arrangement: desks in rows.

The New Paradigm
- Journals.
- Various colored pens and markers.
- Paperback books.
- Portfolios.
- Videocassette tape.
- Computer disk.
- Class arrangement: tables, bean bags, computers.

9

Groups get a charge from flash cube illusion

Participants are literally energized in Phillip Jares' flash cube exercise, which works with any number of people — and works best on carpet.

Purchase a box of disposable flash cubes. They must be the squares that flash four times. (The taller bar flashes will not work.)

On the bottom of each flash cube are four curved slots. Across the middle of each slot, inside the flash cube, is a very thin piece of wire. That wire is the trigger which ignites the flash. Anything that presses against the wire will cause one of the four flashes to ignite.

Use a scissors to cut a wedge off the end of a pencil eraser. This makes an excellent "button" for setting off a flash. Insert the wedge into one of the slots, but don't press it until you have positioned the exercise, which creates an effective (if illusionary) illustration of the power of teamwork.

Ask participants to stand in a circle and hold hands. Stand in the center, making it clear you must be careful not to touch anyone, and instruct them to shuffle their feet rapidly. Hold the flash cube between your finger and thumb. After about a minute, reach out and make contact with someone in the circle.

At the same time, press the "button." The lesson of this trick, of course, is that working together we can accomplish things that seem (and, in fact are) impossible to achieve alone.

The cube trick also works as a "magic volunteer finder." Simply move among attendees, holding out the cube like a divining tool of some sort. Ignite the flash, choosing — seemingly randomly — the next volunteer. A single cube can be used four times for either trick.

10

'Toolbox' of resources provides effective job aids

A resource "toolbox" plays a major role in driving home learning points in training classes delivered by Judith Albers, director of training at NBD Bank in Merrillville, IN.

At the beginning of a customer service class for bank tellers, Albers places a large cardboard box labeled "Tools" at the front of the class. Periodically during the session, she reaches into the toolbox and shows the class a resource they have at their disposal on the job to solve customers' problems or make atonement. Here are a few examples of tools and how they're used:

• Giveaways: Candy or company merchandise to give to disgruntled customers.

• Support: A list of all phone numbers tellers can call for help.

• Stress Relievers: Gag "tools," such as aspirin, antacid, squirt guns, or a kite for those customers you'd like to tell, "Go fly a kite!"

• Computer Aids: Keyboard "helps" that slip onto tellers' keyboards and list the most commonly used functions.

Albers says the toolbox also visually demonstrates how the company supports training skills back on the job.

Donna Loughridge, a systems trainer with MCI Telecommunications in Colorado Springs, CO, puts a colorful spin on new-employee orientation training with plastic Easter eggs. She writes questions on small pieces of paper, then slips them inside eggs, and hides the eggs in a common area — such as the cafeteria — and asks participants to hunt for them.

When an employee finds an egg, the mission is to answer the question inside. This often requires the finder to locate a particular person or department within the company. For example, if the question is, "How many employees work in the packaging area?" the seeker will have to speak to someone working in that area, possibly the supervisor. This, Loughridge says, creates a familiarity with where various people and functions are located, while helping the new associate learn some names and faces.

After finding an answer, the employee returns to the egg-hunt area to find another egg. After all the eggs have been found and the corresponding questions answered, Loughridge asks participants to share their newfound knowledge with the group.

11

'Egg hunt' introduces new employees to company

Energize trainees while dividing them into groups

To reenergize (and reorganize) a group after lunch, Mary Hoppe, a training consultant from Lincoln, NE, gives each returning participant a piece from one of several puzzles she's created using recognizable images like Mount Rushmore, James Dean, or a Coca-Cola logo. The puzzles are made simply by gluing magazine photos to tagboard and cutting them up, Hoppe says.

The class is instructed to find others with pieces that match to form new small groups for the afternoon session. The number of puzzles distributed should match the number of tables in the room. Hoppe distributes a number of pieces from each puzzle equal to the intended size of each small group.

If there are only enough participants for groups of four but the puzzles consist of six pieces each, she places the remaining two pieces of each at the center of a different table; once the group has found its members, they seat themselves at the table where they find their missing pieces.

The activity usually spawns conversation and restores some of the energy lost during the break.

Once Jo-Ann Samo, a program designer with the Federal Business Development Bank in Montreal, Quebec, introduces herself and outlines the objectives of her session, she pulls out a large box of Kleenex. She chooses a participant and hands over the box, asking the participant to pull out as many tissues as she'd like for the exercise, and then pass the box on. Naturally, participants will demand more information to base their Kleenex-pulling decisions on. Tell them they'll be given full instructions only after everyone has pulled the number of tissues they want, Samo says.

When all are done, tell trainees that for every tissue they've pulled, they must reveal a piece of information about themselves — personal or work-related. For example, job titles, how long they've worked at their company, likes or dislikes concerning work, outside hobbies, and so on.

The opener can also be used to lead into training content. For instance, when Samo is delivering time-management seminars, she asks participants to use the tissues to reveal time management problems they have, or make suggestions on how to solve them.

13

Kleenex-pulling activity puts twist on introductions

14

Toys decrease stress, increase creativity

Barbara Stradley, director of staff development at Texas Scottish Rite Hospital for Children, Dallas, TX, brings toys to her training classes.

Her toys include Squish balls, Slinkies, Nerf toys (flying disks, footballs), water toys and games, Rubik's Cubes, puzzles, squirt guns, Koosh balls, and worry stones.

They're great for decreasing stress in classes and meetings, helping tactile learners learn, and increasing creativity, she says.

She leaves the class during the course of the day for a short while, giving attendees "permission" to quietly play. She also leaves the toys out throughout some training sessions or meetings, so participants have ready access.

Stradley says playing makes for a more interesting break than the usual restroom-and-chat scenario and demonstrates that unconventional thinking is welcome in her classroom.

Encouraging creative problem-solving is the focus of Mary Prod's puzzle exercise. Prod, a training coordinator with the California State Dept. of Health, Davis, CA, splits her class into groups of five to seven participants and gives each group a plastic bag containing pieces for a simple 20- to 30-piece puzzle — less two pieces of each, which she keeps herself. She then announces the objective: "The first group that provides me with a complete picture wins."

As the groups assemble their puzzles, they see gaps left by the missing pieces. Typically, Prod says, they check to see if missing pieces are among other groups' pieces. Finding nothing, groups come to her requesting the missing pieces. She calmly restates the objective: "The first group that provides me with a complete picture wins."

For lack of any *normal* solution, someone eventually thinks of a secondary way of meeting the objective: By placing a sheet of paper under the puzzle and drawing in the missing parts, the group "provides a complete picture." The members of the first group to realize that (or to come up with another solution that works) win small prizes.

Unexpected outcome encourages trainees to take initiative

A bridge serves as a metaphor for teamwork, thinking "outside the box," and efficient execution of tasks in classes led by Steven Bundy, manager of training and development, Bosart Co., Springfield, OH.

Bundy draws two bridge standards on opposite sides of a large piece of poster paper. The bridge deck itself is slowly built with attendee ideas that are related to class material, written on Post-it notes and handed to Bundy, who sticks them on the poster with the promise that if the bridge is "finished" before the end of the day, the class will earn a reward.

But Bundy intentionally makes the bridge come up short by "building" it in an arc that will almost, but not quite, reach the other side. As the day goes on, one or more attendees usually point out the bridge's flaw and are allowed to straighten the deck.

Built in an arc, the deck (made of trainee ideas) will not quite reach the other side. Once a trainee takes the initiative to straighten the deck, the Post-its will reach the other side.

To help improve communication skills and raise consciousness about treating customers with empathy, Andy Oman, training and development administrator for Hoffman Engineering, Anoka, MN, uses an exercise featuring a blindfold and Lego toys.

He first has his entire class study a pre-constructed Lego model, often in the form of a plane or house, for one minute. Then one participant in a group of five to seven is blindfolded while other members disassemble the model. Using a photo of the model as a reference, group members instruct the blindfolded participant in reconstructing the model. No handing of pieces to the blindfolded member is allowed. A typical command would be: "Feel for the two-inch wide tile and place at the far left corner." Oman allows two to four minutes for assembly.

To tie this activity to learning, he makes the point that new levels of understanding and communication skills are necessary for dealing with growing demands of internal and external customers.

17

Good listening skills necessary in blindfold exercise

18

Collect simple games for quick energizers

Learning opportunities come in all sizes, shapes, and flavors, says Sheila Devereaux. They also come in boxes, bags, and cartons. That's why she never throws away old cereal boxes, lunch bags, or lunch-size milk cartons. After breaks, Devereaux, a senior management development consultant with the Public Service Electric and Gas Co. in Newark, NJ, uses the games, riddles, puzzles, and brainteasers printed on them to stimulate or re-energize attendees. The participant with the first completed game or puzzle receives a reward.

In her diversity training classes, Kristina Kammerer uses a large map to demonstrate differences and similarities among people.

Kammerer, a training consultant with Allstate Insurance Co. in Irving, TX, posts a plastic-coated map, about 3 x 5 feet, at the front of class. She has each trainee mark with a different colored marker on the map where they were born, and then draw a line connecting all the places they have lived, in order. As they trace their histories, they explain a little about themselves and what they did in each place.

"Oftentimes people find it gives them something in common with other trainees who they didn't feel they had anything in common with," Kammerer says, while helping participants get to know one another beyond name and job title.

19

Searching for similarities among trainees builds bonds

20

Creative thinking simplifies arduous tasks

Toys are a staple in most training rooms. To challenge participants to think creatively and work smarter, Pam Wooldridge, a training specialist for Strouds, City of Industry, CA, enlists the help of a toy paddle with a ball attached to it by a rubber string.

At the end of a day or a learning unit, she asks for a volunteer to review a set of points made in class *while keeping the ball in motion*. Most try to bounce the ball against the paddle, but soon realize that Wooldridge's only stipulation was to keep the ball moving. Soon, she says, participants are swinging the ball until it is wrapped around the paddle, or making it sway back and forth like a pendulum.

After the review, Wooldridge makes the point that the exercise shows people often try to make a task more difficult than it needs to be, and that by thinking creatively they can come up with better ways of doing things.

The exercise can also be used as a session opener or energizer, with participants instructed to keep the ball in motion while they introduce themselves. Again, the exercise ultimately teaches them to work smarter.

To introduce participants to each other, Laura Martell-Boinske, an education and training specialist with Martin Marietta in King of Prussia, PA, gives each person in her training seminars a can of Play-Doh when they arrive for training (it works best if there are chunks of different colors in each can). The group is then instructed to form something out of the dough that in some way represents them. Martell-Boinske emphasizes that the sculpture can be anything.

At each table, participants try to figure out what each sculpture represents. After the guessing is complete, each group member describes what their sculpture actually represents.

The process promotes intimacy between group members because it allows them to learn something unique about each other, she says. It also provides an outlet for fidgety people, as they can play with their dough throughout the session.

21

Play-Doh sculptures illustrate students' unique traits

Effective teams require leadership from all

Marilyn Russell, a nurse educator at the Dallas Medical Resource, Dallas, TX, uses the "rope game" in team-building sessions to stress the importance of achieving the right mix of team members' strengths and limitations to reach desired goals.

Up to nine participants can play the game. A good-size room with all floor obstacles removed is needed. Participants are first asked to put on blindfolds. If a participant refuses, he or she can assume an "observer" role in the game. Then a long nylon rope is tied end-to-end to make a continuous circle. The blindfolded participants are led to the rope and asked to grab it. The trainer then instructs the group to form a triangle with the nylon rope, or some other simple geometric figure. *It's important the trainer provide no other instructions.*

The group must then move together in a way that forms the geometric shape. Natural leaders and followers emerge as the group communicates and configures itself. When the group feels it's made the shape, trainees remove their blindfolds to see how well they have done as a group.

Next, blindfolds go back on as participants are instructed to make another shape. Those emerging as leaders in the first interaction are quietly pulled aside by the trainer and told not to speak. Typically, that silence forces some of those who acted as followers in the first session to assume leadership roles.

Russell then debriefs, stressing that it is only the use of highly effective communication and cooperation that makes forming the shapes possible. "Any team's success depends upon how well each member uses his or her strengths and weaknesses to balance out the team's assets," she says. "A good team-building atmosphere stresses the importance of each member and increases everyone's self-esteem."

23

Magnet visuals make learning stick

Here's a graphic idea that helps better illustrate — particularly for visual learners — sequential concepts or process flows.

To show the relationship of parts to the whole in a tax training course, Joe Seddio, a corporate payroll trainer with Paychex Inc. in Rochester, NY, draws, colors, cuts out, and then laminates the separate pieces illustrating the process flow. He then affixes a sheet of magnet to the back of each piece.

As he begins his session, he attaches each piece of the diagram to a magnetic, dry-erase whiteboard. He then talks about that one piece and its relationship to any other already-revealed pieces. He continues until the entire puzzle/cycle is shown.

During the session, Seddio reveals and removes pieces to create different case studies. He also finds the dry-erase board convenient for writing additional information, jotting down class notes, and demonstrating calculations or other exercises.

Here's an easy-to-make, pocket-size pointer for focusing attention on your transparencies. Bob Johnson, a training consultant with NSW Retail and Wholesale Industry Training Council in Australia, cuts an arrow shape from a business card and turns up about one-half inch of the shaft to make it easier to pick up and position on the point you want to focus on. In addition, the arrow is instantly identifiable and transports easily.

25

Simple pennants instill team spirit

Construction paper pennants reinforce the team attitude in classes facilitated by Leslie Mizerak, a training facilitator at Southern State Community College in Wilmington, OH.

Mizerak posts large baseball-style pennants on classroom walls during courses involving workplace teams. The pennants are labeled with team names and simple slogans. She provides smaller versions for students to pin on their shirts to identify which team they are from during mixed-group activities.

"It may sound childish," she says, "but it helps people feel real team spirit."

This tip from Deb Hartford, a training coordinator for Harris Co., Lincoln, NE, helps prod participants into transferring training skills to the workplace. It works best when trainees have a personal daily planner, either on their desks or one they carry with them during the day.

First you'll need some large, colored dots with an adhesive that allows them to be moved. Give each trainee a few dots. At the end of the session, ask participants to choose the most important learning point they'd like to apply back on the job. Have them write on the dot a few words as a reminder of that new skill/technique. For instance, following training on coaching skills, the dot might say "Ask Questions" as a reminder to not just dole out answers, but to help employees resolve problems by posing questions that will guide them to solutions.

Hartford asks trainees to put their dots in their daily planners on the last day of class, and then move them forward daily in the planner for the next 21 days. She chooses three weeks, she says, because research has shown it takes at least that amount of time to change or acquire a habit.

26

Reminder dots reinforce learning back on the job

'Twine chain' shows ripple effect of individual actions

To demonstrate the effect of one person's actions on others for team-building or leadership courses, Becky Schaefer, a manager of employee involvement at US West, Denver, uses this exercise:

She divides students into small groups and gives one person in each group a ball of twine. That person holds onto the end and passes the ball to another team member, and so on, until everyone holds the strand at some point — keeping it taut without breaking it. Participants are encouraged to loop the twine around a person or two to further complicate the equation, then return the ball to the first person to complete the circuit.

The teams are then asked to experiment with movement. What happens when one person moves her hand to the left two feet? If someone sits down? What sort of cooperation is necessary for the group to move across the room while keeping the string taut without breaking it.

After several minutes, Schaefer asks what was learned. Did the string ever break? If so, why? Were some people forceful while others were accommodating? Did leaders develop? Too many of them? What kinds of communication worked?

Like most training budgets, Janna Bertholf's doesn't provide for the purchase of classroom prizes. But Bertholf, a quality assurance analyst for St. Luke's Episcopal Hospital, Houston, says other departments in the organization can be great resources for finding little trinkets to use as giveaways.

Specifically, Bertholf asks the public affairs department for any leftover promotional items it may have. "It's been a valuable resource for company keychains, magnets, sports bottles, and bags with the company name on them," she says. "All of which make wonderful training prizes."

28

Tap other departments for cost-effective prizes

29

Simple chemical experiment shows value of conflict

A simple demonstration makes a concept crystal clear to participants in T.J. Titcomb's team-building/conflict resolution classes.

Titcomb, director of training at Family Service, Lancaster, PA, begins the class with a discussion on the need to change expectations about conflict. Rather than assuming conflict is only negative, she strives to teach participants to see it as a motivator for change and a tool to ensure all major viewpoints are considered.

Titcomb sets up these supplies at the front of the class: three transparent glass beakers or test tubes filled with water, small packets of sugar and salt, and colored glass marbles. She then demonstrates the difference between "soluble" (solvable) conflicts and "insoluble" (unsolvable) conflicts.

"Any conflict," she explains, "has two distinct viewpoints. Some conflicts are 'soluble.' The two parts combine, they don't disappear — they become something new, keeping the best of both." (She pours a small amount of sugar into a beaker of water and shakes it.)

"Some conflicts are sweet because they are easily resolved through collaboration." (She pours a small amount of salt into the second beaker of water and shakes it.)

"Other conflicts add spice to life. They are a little harder and take more effort to resolve. In time they may reappear again as the two parts separate. We may have to return later and work at them again to keep them soluble." (She shakes the beaker a second time.)

(She then holds up the third water beaker, drops in a glass marble, and shakes it.) "But we must also recognize that some conflicts cannot be resolved. What can we do when faced with insoluble conflicts? They can be understood, appreciated, and accepted. We step back and admire the diversity of ideas, opinions, and values among human beings. We learn that different is okay. We also decide as individuals when to stop trying to force solutions onto insoluble conflicts. *We are then free to put our energy into changing our reaction to people and situations.*"

Titcomb gives each participant a marble as a reminder of the learning point of the class.

30

Taste test teaches meaning of product value

Sandy Freeman, a retail trainer with First Federal Savings Bank in La Crosse, WI, uses this exercise in sales training classes to emphasize that in customers' eyes, "product value" means more than just an equitable price. Depending on situation and need, customers have widely differing expectations of products and services that salespeople need to address.

After a short introduction she asks her participants to take part in a "taste test." Freeman then hands out a "Samplers Taste Test Sheet" and three different samples of candy — chocolate truffles, chocolate mints, and bite-size Tootsie Rolls — asking each participant to comment on quality and taste of each. She then asks all to choose their favorites; most students pick the truffles.

Freeman then provides them with the following information on cost and packaging of the candy:

• Sample A, the truffles, cost $7 for seven pieces and come in a dull gray box.

• Sample B, the mints, cost $6 per pound and come in a foil-wrapped gift box with a card.

• Sample C, the Tootsie Rolls, cost $2.29 for 16 ounces and come in a plastic bag.

Given that information, participants are then asked which candy they would purchase in the following situations (these can be changed to fit the diversity of the group):

(1) Which would you purchase as a gift for your mother-in-law?

(2) Which would you purchase to send with your six-year-old to school as a treat?

(3) Which would you purchase for your spouse to celebrate a big promotion?

Freeman says it typically surprises everyone how small a role price plays in their decision to buy one candy over another. "It's all the factors taken together that influence buying decisions — a good lesson for new salespeople," she says.

Depending on the group and its need for reinforcement, Freeman changes information given about the products to test price tolerance in each of the three scenarios. She then makes that point that desired results or needs change the perception of value.

'Wanted' posters of trainees break the ice

Students in training courses conducted by Craig Hauser and Dale Morehouse, staff members of training and development at Walt Disney World, Orlando, FL, get to know one another via "wanted" posters.

Upon arrival, the trainer gives attendees a sheet like the one below, and asks them to fill it out. After trainees complete the forms, the trainer tapes the posters to a wall. Participants are then asked to read the posters and mark at the bottom of each one who they think it describes.

The trainer, meanwhile, asks each

WANTED

Front mug shot		Side mug shot

Background (information about family, place of birth, career information):
_____
_____

Known behaviors (hobbies): _____
_____

Other points of interest (i.e. "car last seen in" or "known to watch the following TV programs"): _____
_____

participant to pose for two Polaroid photos. The shots are taken against the backdrop of a height marker similar to those shown in actual mug shots. Instead of holding a serial number, participants create tagboard signs displaying their first names and any "known alias," i.e. "Nancy a.k.a. The Accountant."

The instructor then asks students to tape their photos in the appropriate places on their posters.

Reminder goads learners to use training

A recurring problem with training is a lack of on-the-job follow up or action planning. To remind trainees not to forget training once on the job, Miriam Wolf, training coordinator for Children's Bureau in Los Angeles, created a catchy job aid.

She calls it "The Round Tuit." It's actually a round circle of paper or a small pin with the word "Tuit" in the middle. "It's designed for those people who say they're going to implement new training skills or knowledge, but never '*get around to it*,'" Wolf says.

TUIT

She hands out these small reminders to trainees to take back to their jobs, or to reproduce for others. They serve to jog memories long after training classes end, she says.

Trainers recognize participants' performances in class fairly regularly, says D. Bruce Lucier, organizational development and training manager for the City of Fort Lauderdale, FL. But peer recognition is often overlooked. He encourages attendees to compliment classmates freely and frequently, using helium balloons and markers as the medium.

Lucier attaches light-colored balloons to the center of each table following a break. He places markers on each table, and encourages attendees to write on the balloons things done well by other group members.

Lucier says the things most often recognized are the "little things" that make a big difference in the way the group functions, including comments like: friendly coworker, always willing to help, willing to go the extra mile, takes pride in work, caring supervisor, and so forth.

At the end of class, Lucier collects the balloons and asks each participant to comment on what they wrote. He separates comments by theme — pride, customer service, caring, enthusiasm, and so forth — so participants can see clearly the sorts of traits people appreciate in a working environment.

33

Balloon messages let trainees compliment each other

Raise trainees' awareness about disabled workers

Compliance with the Americans with Disabilities Act (ADA), does not mean companies must train employees about the legislation's complex facets. But many organizations have elected at least to raise the awareness of their workforces about working with the disabled population.

Niki Nichols, a trainer with the employee education department at Scott & White Hospital, Temple, TX, accomplishes that goal by using a "boardwalk" exercise that touches on ADA issues in diversity classes. Nichols made the boardwalk from two, four-foot 2x4s connected by a five-inch wide strip of plywood (see illustration on the opposite page). Here's how it works:

Nichols asks for three or four volunteers to stand side-by-side on the narrow boardwalk, letting them know they will be asked to touch and be touched by others. Once everyone is standing on the board, the volunteers are asked to reverse their "left to right" order without touching the floor. Participants who lose their balance and touch the floor are blindfolded. Whoever touches the floor a second time loses the use of one hand (by putting it behind their back or in their pocket). The consequence of a third stumble is the loss of speech. Other restrictions can be applied if there are more falls (ear plugs, loss of the other hand, and so on).

When the new order on the board is established, nearly everyone has had a restriction imposed. Nichols then asks each volunteer to articulate the special challenges the restrictions posed and how they reacted to those losses. She also asks attendees who did not walk the plank if they noticed any differences in the volunteers' interactions as the restrictions mounted.

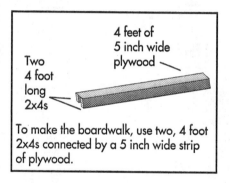

To make the boardwalk, use two, 4 foot 2x4s connected by a 5 inch wide strip of plywood.

35

Silly rewards encourage trainees to take risks

To encourage student participation, Steven Tehovnik, a technical trainer with Legent Corp., Pittsburgh, rewards every volunteered answer, whether right, wrong, or just plain off-base.

Correct answers earn the contributor a roll of Smarties candies. Wrong ones merit a Dum Dum sucker. For the folks just plain lost and floundering, Life Savers.

The technique may sound as if it discourages comments from people afraid of earning a Dum Dum or Life Saver, but if used in a lighthearted way from the course's outset, people enjoy it and take risks, knowing a treat awaits them in any case, Tehovnik says.

Suzanne Allen, health education specialist with Kapiolani Health Care System in Honolulu, uses a common carry-out food box from a restaurant as a prop to encourage trainees to apply their new knowledge or skills back on the job.

At the end of a training day or course, Allen displays a carry-out box and tells the class that there are several options they have when they get a "doggy bag" for their leftovers at a restaurant. She says: "Upon leaving a diner, you could forget the box on the table and never enjoy the food. You could take it home, stick it in the refrigerator, and then forget about it until it is not good anymore. You could take it home and announce to your family, 'This box is mine; don't touch it.' Or you could take the box home and show the contents to the family and encourage them to enjoy the food."

Allen then opens the carry-out box and leads into the review by saying, "The last option is the one I hope you choose today — to share your handouts at home." She then takes out pieces of colored paper cut into food shapes, each with a learning point written on it, and discusses them.

Prop encourages trainees to 'carry-out' learning

37

Fight the notion that 'a little bit of waste' is OK

In departmental quality training sessions that include a module on waste and cost reduction, Bruce Mothes, a value engineer and trainer for Transportation Manufacturing Co. in Roswell, NM, uses the following exercise as a way to combat the notion that "just a little bit of waste" is acceptable.

After talking about saving money and the various ways that even the little things can help or hinder, Mothes removes a crisp $1 bill from his pocket and says it represents a day's worth of waste in the department he's speaking to. He then tears the bill in half, puts the pieces together, and tears them again and again. "Chances are, you won't get too many people excited," Mothes says.

He then removes a $20 bill from his pocket and announces it represents 20 days worth of waste in the department. "That's when interest is piqued," Mothes says. "They *know* you won't rip up a $20 bill."

But rip it he does. "If you have a microphone, tear the bill along its length — nice and slowly — next to the mike so it makes a lot of noise. Then tear it again. You'll hear gasps and groans."

Mothes then asks the group why they were upset with the $20 bill being torn, but not the $1 bill. After a few responses he points out that there are many $1 wastes in the company — enough to equal many, many $20 wastes. "It encourages them to worry about the little wastes just as much as the big wastes," says Mothes.

Editor's Note: Mothes *does* exchange the torn bills for fresh ones. According to the Federal Reserve Bank in Minneapolis, a torn bill can be exchanged at any bank if all its pieces are present or if any single piece is "clearly greater than half" of the original bill.

May Akamine, director of outpatient services and chief nursing officer at Castle Medical Center in Kailua, HI, uses this "tug of war" activity to teach her trainees the importance of clear communication and the dangers of relying on preconceptions.

To set up the activity, you need tape, four long pieces of light, sturdy rope or clothesline (at least 10 feet in length), a sturdy metal ring, and a red scarf or similar bright marker. In the middle of the space for the activity, use tape to mark a 1 foot square. Tie the scarf and one end of each rope to the ring. Place the ring in the middle of the taped-off square with the ropes extended out in four directions (see the diagram on the opposite page).

Divide the class into four teams and have each team hold onto a rope. Give the teams these guidelines: "The purpose of this activity is to get as many points as possible in 30 seconds. A point is scored each time the marker crosses a line. You have 30 seconds to talk about it."

When the "competition" begins, Akamine says the teams usually start tugging at the rope in an attempt to get points for their own teams. After 30 seconds, she asks them how many points they have.

The teams usually have few or no points. Akamine repeats the activity, restating the guidelines again very explicitly. Usually, she says, the teams start to ask more pointed questions about the purpose of the activity. The teams eventually realize that the activity is a cooperative effort not a competition, and that they must work together to pile up points by moving the scarf rapidly in a circle over the taped box.

Following the activity, Akamine discusses clear communication, the danger of making assumptions, competition versus cooperation, and teamwork concepts.

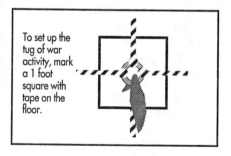

To set up the tug of war activity, mark a 1 foot square with tape on the floor.

39

Diversity goes beyond race and gender

Here's an inexpensive way to demonstrate diversity in the workplace:

People tend to think of diversity in terms of race or gender, overlooking the less obvious differences, such as age, geographic background, and so on, says Sharon Lovoy, president of Lovoy's Team Works, Birmingham, AL. She starts diversity training sessions with an exercise designed to help people recognize that every individual is unique, and that diversity issues often go beyond the obvious.

She pairs off participants and asks them to work with their partners to list the differences between them — hair color, education level, state of birth, and whatever else they notice.

After two or three minutes, Lovoy stops the exercise and locates the team with the longest list. She has one of them read their list to the class. Their prize is a box each of "multicultural" Crayola crayons. (The special set, containing eight colors that can be used to create a multitude of skin tones, is available for 89 cents per box through Chaselle Inc., 800-242-7355).

George Wilson, principal training specialist, Florida Power & Light, North Palm Beach, FL, uses jellybeans to demonstrate the extent of diversity within small work groups. He sets 25 plastic cups on a large table. Each cup contains a different flavor of jellybean. In front of each cup is an index card labeled with a distinct demographic or human characteristic reflecting differences in ethnicity, gender, age, place of birth, or personality type. For example: Born in the Northeast, under 25 years old, outgoing/expressive, has African roots, detail-oriented thinker.

At an appropriate point in the session, ideally just before an afternoon break, attendees are given small paper cups and instructed to visit the display and take one jellybean from each cup that reflects a characteristic that is present in their work group.

After counting their jellybeans and recording the number, participants may enjoy them as a snack. After the break, Wilson leads a discussion on workforce diversity and how to help diversity thrive, using the jellybean exercise to demonstrate the diversity that exists even in very small groups.

40

Jellybean exercise reflects diversity within groups

41

Ta-Ka-Radi block game livens up review sessions

Here's how to effectively use a simple prop — children's building blocks — to review:

Especially when particularly dry material is involved, Sherri Williams, technical instructor at Philip Morris USA, Richmond, VA, livens up review sessions with blocks from a game called Ta-Ka-Radi, but she says any rectangular blocks will work.

First she arranges the blocks in a tower by placing three side-by-side on a desk or table, then laying three more at right angles across those, and so on until all the blocks are used and they create a tower that is at least five sets high.

A player earns the right to take a block from any layer of the tower except the top one by correctly answering a review question. The game ends when the tower falls or when only one layer of blocks is left, whichever comes first. The player with the most blocks wins, as long as that player hasn't toppled the tower.

Renee Collins, a trainer with Grainger Co. in Cincinnati, OH, uses all the tools at her disposal — literally — when teaching coaching skills to managers and supervisors.

Each group of three to four participants in her classes receives a toolbox, including a six-piece wrench set and six nuts of varying sizes. Each nut has a case study or performance situation attached to it that requires a particular response on the part of managers. Collins calls these, appropriately enough, "nut cases." Each wrench has an accompanying coaching skill taped to it. For example, skills such as praising, redirecting, constructively criticizing, negotiating, or resolving conflict.

Participants then choose a nut with its companion case study, read it, and determine which wrench (coaching skill) to apply to address it best. For example, participants might get a situation where an employee is promoted into a new job and needs reassuring because of initial uncertainty. In this case, "praising" is the right coaching choice. Participants confirm if their choice is correct by seeing if the wrench size they choose fits the nut. Collins says they also act out the coaching skill.

42

Clever use of tools as props builds coaching skills

Help trainees think positive about meeting team goals

A Hula Hoop doubles as a fun and effective teaching tool for participants in Jack Norwood's classes. Norwood says this activity — which is based on an old party game — helps get a class loosened up and better acquainted, while building teamwork among participants.

Norwood, internal organizational developmental consultant with US West, Denver, has the class form a circle and hold hands, then places a Hula Hoop somewhere in the circle so that two people are holding hands through the hoop. He asks group members to estimate how long they think it will take to get the hoop around the circle — without anyone letting go of hands. He says the group usually estimates much longer than it actually takes.

After the activity, Norwood discusses goal setting and how the group's perception of what they thought they could achieve fell short of what they actually achieved. He reminds the group not to downplay their ability to succeed when setting goals — as a team and individually.

Norwood then places a second, smaller hoop at the opposite side of the circle and tells the group that the two hoops must go around the circle in opposite directions without anyone in the group letting go of hands. He has the group determine how much time they think the activity will take. Once again, they usually overestimate the time it takes to complete the activity.

After the activity, he debriefs the group on their success in working together as a team, pointing out how positive encouragement from other team members and good communication helped move the hoop through the circle faster.

44

Toy eggs energize review sessions

Plastic, colored Easter eggs are used to make review sessions more fun in Ann Hensel's courses.

Hensel, an instructor at Discover Card Services Inc., Columbus, OH, asks each participant near the end of the session to compile a list of four or five questions and answers related to the course material, using notes or other resources.

She inserts slips of paper numbered according to class size inside the eggs, and gives each student an egg.

She asks participants to sit in a circle, and one person is selected to begin the review by tossing an egg to someone else. The person who throws the egg then asks a question. If the recipient answers correctly, he or she keeps the egg that was thrown, tosses the other to another person, and asks a different question. If, however, a participant fails to answer correctly, the egg is tossed back to its original owner, who throws it to someone else and asks the same question.

When everyone — time permitting — has had a chance to participate, Hensel stops the game, has students open their eggs, and gives them a prize that matches the number they find in the eggs.

To demonstrate the importance of listening skills in dealing with customers via telephone, Shari Petrak, a liability claims training specialist, Nationwide Insurance, Columbus, OH, pairs off participants and designates one person in each pair as the "sender" and the other as the "receiver."

The sender is given a diagram showing a configuration of 10 dominoes. The receiver gets a matching set of dominoes. A barrier such as a notebook is placed between the two. The sender's job is to verbally communicate the pattern shown on her diagram to the receiver, who tries to duplicate it. The sender is not permitted to see the receiver's work. Petrak allows six to eight minutes for the exercise, depending on the complexity of the arrangements.

She follows up with a discussion of barriers to clear communication, such as using terms unfamiliar to the other person, giving instructions too rapidly, or failing to listen carefully to questions.

45

Duplicating domino patterns builds listening skills

46

Intriguing incentives improve class participation

To stress to trainees that they are the "keys" to the success of their respective companies — no matter what their job titles or pay levels — Judy Westrich, a customer service manager with Bass Pro Shops in Springfield, MO, hands them an old key each time they answer a question in class. Trainees are given no hint as to the purpose of the keys, but at the end of class the participant with the most keys wins a small prize.

As Westrich collects the keys at the end of the class, she reinforces the message and gives each participant a new key ring, asking them to share with her the most valuable lessons they have learned.

Catherine Dux, manager of education and development at Alberta Motor Association in Edmonton, Alberta, Canada, encourages participants to send a thank-you note to the person responsible for authorizing them to attend her training courses (usually supervisors). She says this ensures supervisors know their approval is appreciated and that the course was completed.

Dux suggests participants include in the thank-you an invitation to meet later to briefly discuss what they learned and how they will use the training back on the job.

47

Participant thank-you notes serve multiple purposes

48

'Whip' reminds students not to downplay their skills

People often are unaware of how they "beat up on themselves" during a session, says Patti Lovaas, a training specialist for the Social Security Administration, Denver. They do things like apologizing for their answer to a question, by saying things like "I'm no expert but..." before offering input, or by saying they don't have enough experience to contribute meaningfully.

To make people aware of that behavior, Lovaas brings a whip to class (a wooden dowel with colorful strips of plastic attached to one end). She assigns someone to be the "keeper of the whip." When that person hears anyone in the room saying or implying derogatory things about themselves or anyone else, the keeper passes the whip to the offender, as a reminder of the "beating" that person is dishing out. Lovaas got her "whip" from a magic store, but most craft stores carry the items necessary to make one.

Perhaps nothing distracts students more thoroughly than a room that's too hot or muggy, says Bob Cooper, an administrative analyst for the U.S. Bancruptcy Court, San Diego. But if classrooms with little or no air conditioning are a fact of life, there's a way to improve the comfort factor while delivering a message, he says.

Cooper uses his computer to design and print small cards — about six inches square — on heavy paper, and staples the cards to tongue depressors or large ice cream sticks to create small hand fans. Each fan is imprinted with a message related to the course topic, such as "Data processing is a breeze," or "Writing reports is a breeze."

49

Hand fans double as topic reminders

50

Openers bring out trainees' personalities in novel ways

Here's an ice breaker designed to work with groups of attendees who already know one another:

At the outset of class, E. Joy Antolini, a human resources associate for Harrah's in Atlantic City, NJ, asks participants to write a name on their badges that represents their alter egos. Instead of John Smith and Mary Jones, Antolini's classroom is populated by Napoleon, Charlie Brown, the Cowardly Lion, and Albert Einstein. Then attendees explain why they chose those names.

• In another exercise, Janice Pawlik, a training assistant for Progressive Insurance Co., Mayfield Heights, OH, gives participants scissors, glue, and a large stack of old magazines. She then asks each attendee to draw the name of another trainee from a hat and create a quick collage of pictures and words that describe that coworker. Introductions are more personalized this way, Pawlik says, as attendees explain why they chose certain pieces of the collage.

To make taking final tests a little more enjoyable, Jan Schamp, a trainer at Midland Mortgage Co., Oklahoma City, lets trainees roll the dice to determine which test questions they must answer.

Schamp makes her final test very long — 60 to 70 questions divided into sections of at least six questions. Trainees roll a die labeled with test sections to determine the two sections from which to answer questions. Then they roll a regular, numbered die to determine how many questions in those sections to select and answer. Depending on the rolls, a trainee can have a maximum of 12 questions or a minimum of two questions to answer.

51

Rolling dice determines trainees' test questions

52

Lemons sharpen trainees' observation skills

To sharpen participants' observation skills — and to illustrate that no observation is too small or insignificant — Sherry Miller, director of staff development assistant at the Hi-Desert Continuing Care Center, Joshua Tree, CA, employs a bunch of lemons.

She greets students at the door as they arrive for class and hands everyone a lemon from a bucket with the instructions, "Get to know your lemon. Observe it closely, but don't write on it or otherwise deface it." Miller herself participates in the exercise by picking a lemon before anyone arrives and secretly injecting it with red food dye to drive home a point she makes later that day.

Near the end of the day, Miller collects all the lemons, mixes them together in the bucket, and asks attendees to attempt to pick out "their" lemons. When everyone is confident they have retrieved the lemon with which they started the day (including Miller), she concludes the exercise by telling the class that no matter how small the observation, it is always worth noting because you never know what might be going on beneath the surface. She then slices her lemon open to reveal the red dye.

If you have something lengthy for students to learn — a mission statement, a set of objectives, a detailed safety procedure — try writing the steps on cardstock, cutting it up, and dumping the pieces on a large table, says Krista Hartjen, a member of the career development staff at OUM & Associates, Bellevue, WA. Then ask participants to put the pieces back in order. The process makes the task of memorizing less tedious, and allows group members to work together to solve problems.

53

Puzzles simplify complex models

Goldfish activity teaches myriad skills

In multiweek sessions, Letty Corredera, a trainer with Aetna Life Insurance, Allentown, PA, uses goldfish as an inexpensive way to teach such myriad skills as communication, adaptability, leadership, management of resources, and teamwork.

Supplies needed include two healthy goldfish, a medium-sized fish bowl, some decorative seashells and rocks, fish food, and an aquarium net.

Students are grouped in pairs or trios and each is assigned a time period when they are responsible for the health and well-being of the fish. For example, during a six-week course, 18 students are divided into groups of three. Each group is responsible for caring for the fish for a week. Responsibilities include feeding the fish twice daily and changing the water at the end of the week.

Among the lessons learned are:

• Leadership. A group leader must designate the division of duties.

• Management of resources. Individuals must record their duties. Food supplies also must be maintained.

• Teamwork. Group members are instructed to help one another remember their duties.

• Adaptability. Groups may need to work around the absence of team members.

• Communication. Information about when and how much to feed the fish must be shared for consistency.

• Time management. Each group is instructed to clean the fish bowl in 20 minutes or less.

At the end of the training program, Corredera uses this mnemonic device to drive home the message:

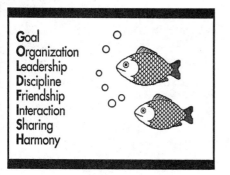

Goal
Organization
Leadership
Discipline
Friendship
Interaction
Sharing
Harmony

55

'Doodle sheets' keep wandering minds occupied

There's no use fighting it: Even the most attentive students sometimes need to let their minds wander. Kenneth Kuzia, senior human resources development specialist with Rochester Gas and Electric, Rochester, NY, recognizes that reality.

Kuzia hands each student a "doodle sheet," consisting of an 11 x 14 sheet of paper on which he has photocopied a number of doodles representing key learning points from class. The quality of the art is unimportant. The sheet's only purpose is to serve as a sketch pad — and as a tool for keeping course materials in participants' brains at least subliminally.

Lisa Schreiber, president of Novations in Omaha, NE, uses this exercise to help participants explore alternatives to this common workplace problem: *lack of communication + uncertainty + perceived competition = irrational behavior.*

Called "nickel auction," the exercise requires 10 nickels, and starts with five chairs placed at the front of the classroom. Divide the large group into five smaller groups. Ask each group to pool their available pocket change and give it to a designated group representative. Have those five reps come to the front of the room to sit with the other group reps.

Start your nickel auction. In round one, ask each rep — one by one — to "bid" or "pass" on one of the five nickels. Each nickel goes to the highest bidder, and bidding continues until all five nickels are gone. Send the reps back to their groups with the change. Review which groups won bidding contests and how much they paid for each nickel.

Have groups pick new representatives for round two. But this time let the reps have a private discussion together for five minutes. They inevitably decide to each bid one cent for each nickel and allow everyone to get one.

Collaboration triumphs in 'nickel auction'

57

Pennies worth their weight in gold in class

It may be true that you can't buy much with a penny these days, but your Lincoln-heads can be worth their weight in gold in the classroom:

Sonya Porter, an assistant sales manager for Health Partners of Philadelphia, gives attendees two cents each as they sign in for a workshop, and tells them they'll be expected to "put their two cents' worth" into the session. Each time a person volunteers, asks a question, leads a group, or contributes to the class, Porter exchanges one cent for a raffle ticket. At the end of the day she holds a drawing for small prizes. Only those who "put their two cents in" are eligible.

Chuck Murphy, a corporate trainer at Shawmut Bank, Boston, distributes five pennies to each participant at the beginning of class. He tells them management wanted him to distribute their raises in advance, to lighten things up. Then he tells them the real purpose of the coins is a game called "Spend a Penny."

Whenever he asks a question, he explains, he'll use the "first hand up" method of choosing a volunteer to answer. Anyone offering a correct answer gets to spend a penny. The object is to spend all five cents by the end of the day. Anyone who does receives a prize.

The game benefits the class in several ways, Murphy says. It maintains students' attention, allows for ongoing class interaction, provides continuous review of materials, makes the learning experience fun, and recognizes active class participants.

Nothing like money to keep a group's attention

59

Tennis swing illustrates proper follow-through

Judy Clarke, a training officer for American Express, Australia, uses a principle of tennis to demonstrate the importance of follow-through in a session on customer service. Right in the training room she softly hits two tennis balls. On the first, she stops her swing as soon as the racquet contacts the ball. She then hits the second ball with equal force, but follows through on the stroke. The second ball goes considerably farther than the first.

She then lobs tennis balls with "customer service" written on them to each attendee. They keep them until the end of the session as reminders of the importance of "following through" in customer service on customer requests and problems. At the end of class, she has trainees turn the balls in for prizes.

When a course requires attendees to gather and organize a large amount of data, Myron Lieske, a total quality manager for Honeywell, Plymouth, MN, provides each participant with a computer disk or specially designed notebook.

There are two benefits, Lieske says. First, the job aid encourages students to gather complete information, because the instructor has already done some of the work for them. Second, it serves as a guide to the process, making the assignment less formidable.

An example is Lieske's benchmarking workshop where attendees are required to follow certain steps and gather detailed information. Lieske provides a record book to each student, which serves as a guide to the process and a place to keep information. If computers are available to all students, he says, the "books" can be computer disks, designed to contain the same information as the books.

60

Computer disks capture detailed data for reference

61

Ball-throwing simulates how messages are sent

Bill Kennard, vice president of MEI Salons in Cincinnati, OH, uses an aluminum foil ball to visually demonstrate how communication can succeed or break down, depending on how a message is delivered or received.

Before class he inserts a small token — a coin or whistle, for example — inside a ball of foil, folded so the token can be easily removed later. He then adds several more layers to the outside of the ball.

He tells the class that the foil ball is a message, and proceeds to "deliver" the message several different ways, explaining the significance of each mode of delivery as he goes. Examples include:

1. Sender looks at and tosses ball directly to receiver, who then tosses it back in the same way (a direct, clear communication loop).

2. Sender looks at one receiver and tosses to another (the person to whom the message was intended never received it).

3. Sender tosses to a receiver who tears some layers off the ball before passing it on to another receiver (the second receiver gets only a part of the message).

4. Sender tosses the ball with force to a receiver (the receiver gets

defensive or has negative feelings about the way the message was sent).

At the end of the exercise, Kennard folds back the layers of the ball to reveal the "surprise" at the core, demonstrating that the message participants received had a "hidden agenda" — the token.

62

Lottery tickets lure trainees to retain course concepts

Ron Gevaudan, a training specialist at Blue Cross of Western Pennsylvania, Pittsburgh, PA, gives lottery tickets as rewards during training review sessions. At the end of the course, he groups people into threes or fours and reviews with a Trivial Pursuit-like question and answer session, keeping score to find the team with the most correct answers. The next day, Gevaudan picks up Pennsylvania state lottery tickets for the winning team, using each employee's identification number to choose the numbers.

Looking for a way to add a little vitality to courses dealing with technical subject matter? Becky Simonson, a training specialist with Bankers Systems Inc., St. Cloud, MN, uses an "Old West" theme.

The theme permeates every aspect of the presentation. Trainees' invitations arrive in the form of announcements to join the "Posse." The invitations ask attendees to dress in Western wear or jeans and casual shirts. Name tags are shaped like deputies' badges. Materials are printed with typefaces reminiscent of the wild west.

Trainees each receive a deck of playing cards imprinted with their division logo. They might even play a poker hand during breaks.

At scheduled times throughout the day, Simonson gives each attendee a playing card (from a deck not matching the ones provided as attendance prizes). The goal for trainees is to form a winning poker hand. Participants may exchange up to four of their cards if they correctly answer two questions in writing before the afternoon break. Simonson awards a card to anyone who attempts to answer the questions. At break time, the participant with the best poker hand wins a "Western look" photo album.

63

'Old West' theme adds life to dry courses

64

Electronic tips offer ongoing computer training

Sending an electronic "training tip of the week" on a computer network lends an air of interest and anticipation to training topics, says Jean Mitchell-Lanham, an automation specialist with the law firm of Cooley, Godward, Castro, Huddleson & Tatum in San Francisco. She developed the idea for training users of a word-processing program.

Mitchell-Lanham keeps a log of calls to the training department's "hotline support service" for software support, and selects the questions most frequently asked each month. She then develops "tips" from these questions explaining how to perform a word processing feature.

Each week she places a tip on the computer network that appears on users' screens when they log on; there is no way to detour or bypass the tip. If users choose not to read the tip, they can hit the "return" key. Mitchell-Lanham formats tips to pique readers' curiosity. She uses catchy phrasing, subtle humor, bold type, or flashing words to capture users' attention for the short time it takes to read the tip.

The tip never is more than 22 lines, and users also have the option of printing out a copy of the tip.

To teach participants the value of recognizing and addressing the sensitive issue of group dynamics in the workplace, Samantha Doly, staff training officer for the AMP Society, Brisbane, Australia, breaks the class into groups of four or five and assigns each a problem that must be solved by consensus. She tells the groups that while they work on the problem, she will place customized baseball caps on the heads of three attendees in each group. The hats are labeled:

- Know It All — Ignore Me
- Expert — Listen to Me
- Insecure — Encourage Me

Doly instructs group members to treat the people wearing the hats according to the labels, although each person wearing a cap is unaware of what the cap says.

When forced to deal with those dynamics, Doly says, groups rarely reach consensus within the 10-minute time limit she sets. The point of the exercise is to teach participants to be sensitive to differing personalities that might affect a group.

65

Sensitize trainees to different personalities in a group

Lottery-style review plays on gambling appetites

Kaye Sanders, training coordinator with the Jacksonville Electric Authority, Jacksonville, FL, uses people's appetite for lottery games in her review sessions. She includes one of her self-designed lottery tickets in each packet of course materials, or simply tapes a ticket to every desk or chair. A corresponding number to each of the tickets is included in Sanders' large "lottery box."

At review time, Sanders asks each participant to write three or four review questions. She then selects a lottery number from the box and asks the student holding that ticket to answer a question relating to the course material. If he or she needs help, Sanders encourages the group to provide assistance.

Once the question is answered correctly, the person initially selected picks a number from the box and poses a question from his or her list. The lottery continues until everyone in the group has a chance to ask and answer a question. Sanders says trainers should also prepare a list of questions in case a trainee says, "All the questions on my list have been asked."

Painter's caps serve as unique name tags for students in Donna Burdge's classes.

As students arrive at class Burdge, an organizational development trainer with Columbia Hospital Inc., Milwaukee, hands them plain white painters' caps (available at paint stores) and asks them to use markers to write their names prominently on them. Attendees are also encouraged to use pictures and words that describe areas of their lives in which they feel most creative, but to leave a blank space on the cap (about 4 inches x 4 inches). When they finish their hats, Burdge asks them to explain their "creative cap" to at least one person they don't know.

At the end of the workshop, participants are asked to visually describe and share what they have learned or found valuable about the session by filling in the blank space on the cap. This helps provide closure for the workshop and personal expression for participants, Burdge says.

After the workshop, the colorful caps serve as reminders back on the job and spark interest from others.

67

Painters' caps make unique name tags

68

Remind new trainers to keep a sense of humor

At the end of her train-the-trainer sessions, Ann Lieberman, personnel development director at TopValue Markets in Long Beach, CA, unveils her "training survival kit," a bag containing symbolic items that will help trainers survive their upcoming travails. For effect, Lieberman places a red cross on the outside of the kit. The kit contains:

- Pot holder for hot tempers.
- Flower seeds to grow good, positive thoughts.
- Aspirin for unforeseen headaches.
- Life Savers to stimulate creative training ideas for routine sessions.
- Key chain to hold those tried-and-true training techniques.
- Skill cards with tips from the course for security and reminders.
- Adhesive bandages for wounded feelings.

Lieberman makes a production of presenting a kit to each trainee and asks that they not look inside until everyone has a packet. She then pulls each item out of her sample packet and describes its symbolism. "I tell them the items are in recognition of what they'll be doing, which won't be easy but should still be fun. I want them to keep a sense of humor," she says.

Jerry Martin, an instructor in the training and organizational development department, Utah State University, Sandy, UT, uses a potato and a related, well-known toy to send a message to trainees about what kind of audience they need to be to get the most from his sessions.

He opens the class by holding up a large potato and asking participants for the different names for it. Words like "spud" and "tuber" usually come out, but "tator" is the word Martin is looking for.

"With that term in mind," he tells the class, "what kind of tator is this?" He then produces a Mr. Potato Head doll and puts a pair of glasses on the toy. Eventually, attendees come up with the term "spec-tator." He puts the question to the class again after attaching a pair of ears to the doll. The answer, of course, is "ear-tator" (irritator).

Martin then explains that he doesn't want any spectators or irritators in the class. He tells attendees that what he wants are strong "partici-tators." They get the pun, he says, and the tone for class is set.

69

Mr. Potato Head helps set positive tone

70

Challenge teams to create ideas that 'stand up' on their own

This activity suggested by Fanny Lee, a system analyst supervisor at Pacific Gas & Electric, San Francisco, CA, teaches teams to work together to build ideas that stand up against something — a hair dryer in this case.

During a six-month team-building course, Lee uses different colored poker chips to divide the class into teams as participants arrive, with no more than five participants in a team. She then gives each team 50 index cards and encourages team members to write one idea per card that relates to good team-building or teamwork skills during the course.

At the end of the course, Lee tells each team to pick their top 20 idea cards. She gives teams 15 minutes and a roll of tape to build the highest tower they can out of their idea cards. The tower cannot be taped to the table or any other support. At the end of the allotted time, Lee stands six feet from each tower, turns on a blow dryer for 30 seconds, and sees which towers survive. She then rewards the teams with surviving towers.

This technique by Donna Vaughn, a member of the sales and management development staff at South Carolina National Bank, Columbia, SC, encourages inquisitiveness in trainees. She carries extra markers and pens to the classroom in a brightly colored box, which she places in clear view near the front of the room — with a candy bar or other prize inside.

Invariably, someone asks what is in the box. Vaughn praises the person's curiosity and awards the hidden prize. Sometimes she gives the entire group a break. The technique energizes the class, she says, and encourages questioning and openness.

71

Encourage curiosity with candy rewards

72

Fortune cookies lift class mood

Sandy Staton, an employee at Conoco Inc. in Houston, TX, uses fortune cookies to reward participants and to help temper negative attitudes. Chronic complainers in her classes are offered fortune cookie "prizes." They are asked to break open a cookie and read the message to the rest of the class. "Most fortunes have a positive saying, so it lifts the class mood," Staton says. She usually buys 150 cookies for her one-day classes.

This technique is used to reinforce training concepts taught earlier in class. In training new employees, Billie Lott, a training specialist with the Department of Health and Welfare, Caldwell, ID, has them play a guessing game called "Off the Top of Your Head." The centerpiece of the game is a Styrofoam head, the kind used for holding a wig. In one class called "How to Consider Resources for a Food Stamp Household," she sticks small pieces of paper to the head with stick pins. The pieces have different types of resources typed on them, and are pinned so the words are concealed.

One at a time, trainees select a piece of paper from the head, read it to the group, and are then asked to explain agency regulations regarding that resource. Correct explanations are given a point, and the trainee with the most points at the end of the game is the winner.

73

Styrofoam head holds course concepts for review

74

Caps remind managers to be 'Coach'

During managers' training sessions on coaching, Tracie Goulet, a training specialist with Blue Cross, Kansas City, MO, steers the discussion to how infrequently managers wear the "hat" of coach.

As they discuss this concept, Goulet passes out baseball caps, each imprinted with the company logo and "Coach."

The hats are a hit, Goulet says. "The managers usually wear them throughout the class. The hats also help to remind them to take the image of 'managers as coaches' back to the workplace," he says.

As part of an informal needs analysis before class, Pat Carroll, owner of Educational Medical Consultants, Middletown, CT, supplies prospective participants with stickers that match the red, yellow, and green of a traffic light. Participants then use stickers to mark their course preferences or areas of need. Green indicates a topic of interest; yellow, something of questionable value; red, material with little or no application.

The system also can be used at the start of a class, to help the instructor tailor the presentation to the needs of attendees, she says, or for post-course evaluation.

75

Stickers help trainees indicate areas of need

76

'Martian experiment' shows why clear instructions are crucial

Clear communication is crucial to a successful training process, so Dennis Menchella, vice president of training and special projects for Morrison Co., Mobile, AL, uses this exercise in train-the-trainer sessions to focus on providing clear instructions.

To introduce the exercise, Menchella discusses the five levels of learning: (1) *Unconscious Incompetent:* I don't know, and I don't know that I don't know. (2) *Conscious Incompetent:* I know that I don't know. (3) *Conscious Competent:* I know that I can do the task but I have to consciously think through each step. (4) *Unconscious Competent:* I can do the job and I'm not even aware, consciously, of what I need to do to do it. (5) *Conscious Unconscious Competent:* Not only can I perform the job without thinking about it, I can also consciously think through, step by step, what I need to do and explain it to others. (This is the level where he says effective trainers should function.)

The exercise is called "The Martian Experiment," and uses an unopened pack of cigarettes. At the beginning of class he asks how many trainees are smokers and how long they've smoked, trying to identify someone who is a long-time smoker and has reached the level of "unconscious competent." That volunteer is brought to the front of the room and told by the trainer: "I am a Martian and have recently been hired by (brand name) cigarette company as a cigarette tester. I have only a literal knowledge of the English language and I know nothing about smoking a cigarette. You will teach me how to smoke — without using your hands."

Inevitably the volunteer starts with the instruction "*pick up* the pack." Menchella has some fun with this by either picking the pack up with his mouth or by saying, "Hey baby, what are you doing tonight?"

The volunteer instructor continues the process: opening the pack, taking a cigarette out, putting the cigarette in his mouth, etc. Menchella says it's important the trainer deliberately think and act naively — like someone with no knowledge of cigarettes.

At the end of the exercise, review the elements of clear instruction giving. In their own communications and instructions, you want the class to: (1) Be specific. (2) Skip no procedural steps. (3) Clarify any murky instructions.

77

'Babysitting' eggs teaches customer awareness

An egg becomes the customer in an exercise to increase customer focus used by Carla Zilles, a training officer with Telecom of Melbourne, Australia.

The class is split into small groups, each of which is given an egg. The eggs serve as "customers" for the duration of the workshop. Participants are asked to take care of their customers and to keep them involved in all activities — including breaks, eating times, and nighttimes.

The lesson makes two points, says Zilles:

• The customer, like the egg, is fragile and must be handled with extreme care.

• Total and constant customer awareness is necessary to keep customers from defecting to the competition.

Stickers sent with reminder letters to trainees three to six weeks before a course act as visual notice that training is coming up, says Nancy Doody, a trainer with the Department of Navy training center in Restow, VA. Participants receive a brightly colored, peel-off sticker to put on a calendar or appointment book indicating the course title, date, time, and sponsor.

Teamwork
Sept. 22
Training Center
Rm. 1

78

Stickers remind trainees of upcoming training

79

Silly Putty succinctly captures students emotions

Once you give students Silly Putty, they're reluctant to give it up, says Caryl Neimes, manager of noncredit programs at the University of Missouri, Kansas City. Niemes uses the substance to introduce new topics or when she wants to make a point and see students' reactions. Silly Putty acts as a cheap yet effective medium for students to express themselves in the following activities:

During a course on job safety, for example, Neimes gives participants a piece of Silly Putty and tells them to warm it and get the feel of it in their hands. She then briefly describes a worst-case scenario about a job-site accident and asks participants to form the Silly Putty based on their emotions as she speaks. Neimes then has participants describe what they've shaped and how it illustrates their emotions.

Neimes also repeats the exercise by briefly describing a more positive experience, and walks through the room again so participants can discuss their Silly Putty creations and their feelings.

Straws and masking tape are the only tools needed for this simple team-building exercise used by Rocio Escobar, an instructor for Baskin-Robbins in Burbank, CA.

Escobar divides the class into teams and asks each team to build a freestanding structure by taping straws together, but *not* taping anything to the floor, ceiling, or walls. Participants are timed, and the team with the tallest structure gets a prize.

80

Simple team-building activity stresses ingenuity

81

Counterfeit prize money personalizes rewards

Play money is a staple in many training rooms, used to reward attendees who report back from break on time or who actively participate in class. But the next time you're going to use play money to "sell" prizes during your sessions, consider turning counterfeiter like Lisa Slanina, assistant trainer, Rogers Cablesystems, Mississauga, Ontario. Slanina makes her own play money with the help of desktop publishing and the company photocopier, personalizing the fake currency with a picture of the company's CEO.

Poster-sized photos of everyday items stimulate discussion on the importance of perspective, says Don Allison, national sales trainer for Hallmark Cards, Kansas City. Calling his activity the "Power of Imagination," Allison uses photo blow-ups to illustrate how using unique ideas can make basic information more interesting.

The photos are taken at angles that make identifying the objects difficult. The objects are "blown up" larger than life, or show a close-up of only a small part of the subject. Allison's blow-ups include a donut, a turtle shell, an alligator snout, and a piece of grass sticking up out of the snow. Can you guess the example shown below?

He hangs 20 of the posters in the training room and challenges participants to describe what each poster is on entry forms. The reward for getting the most correct answers is a dinner for two.

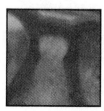

Photos of "blown up" objects show how using unique ideas can make information more interesting.

Answer: The nosepiece of a pair of eyeglasses.

83

Black jack review keeps students involved

Trainees can't help but get involved in the card game "black jack" as played in courses led by Chris McCann, training coordinator with Nationwide Insurance Co., Wallingford, CT.

Each student receives a playing card upon entering the classroom and is instructed to leave the card face down. When McCann asks for volunteers or asks a question during the session, the student who answers or volunteers receives another card (shown face up).

When several students have a set of cards, McCann says, "Let's gamble!" She awards anyone with "black jack" (a face card and an ace) a prize. If the session involves a lot of questioning, she tallies the scores at the end of the day and awards the student with the most "black jacks" a larger prize.

One of the toughest lessons control-minded managers have to learn is delegation. Trainer Jerilyn Willin uses one of the least expensive visual aids available — the balloon — to help managers (especially new managers) lose the "I can do it all myself" mentality. Willin suggests this exercise:

Have one manager come to the front of the room and present him or her with a balloon labeled "budget" or some other task or duty such as "inventory." The manager's task is to keep that balloon aloft by hitting it. No problem. Now add another balloon with a different label. Still no problem. Keep adding balloons with labels. The manager can call "help" at any time and delegate a balloon or two to a fellow attendee. More and more balloons are added until there are enough people involved to keep them all in the air — illustrating the futility of managers trying to do everything by themselves.

84

Juggling challenge shows need for delegation

85

Keeping balloons aloft builds teamwork

The "balloon metaphor" is a favorite closing exercise of Cher Holton, executive director of Holton Consulting Group, Raleigh, NC.

Holton distributes balloons to everyone, and asks them to blow them up and tie knots in them. Their challenge is to form groups and begin batting the balloons into the air, keeping all aloft. There's only one catch: Participants may hit their own balloon only twice consecutively; they have to hit someone else's before hitting their own again. After a minute Holton stops the exercise, and the group discusses what has happened. She asks the group these questions:

"How are these balloons like the members of your team?" Full of hot air, different sizes/shapes/colors, up and down, hard to control, you lose some of them, takes work to keep them together, etc.

"Did all of the balloons stay up at the same rate?" Some balloons, just like some people, are easier to control and deal with than others.

"Can one person keep all of the balloons up alone?" It takes teamwork. Although the group tends to run into each other and step on each others' toes, nobody minds because everyone has been focused on the balloons — the *group* goal.

Here's a creative way to retain student interest that works at the beginning, middle, or end of a session:

Debi Garner, a staff consultant with Meredith Corp., Des Moines, IA, uses a darning needle to extract the fortunes from fortune cookies purchased at a grocery store (this is easier with some brands than with others, she says, and easier than it sounds in any case). She then customizes a message for each and uses the needle to replace the sayings with "fortunes" personalized for each trainee.

If she's using the cookies as an ice breaker, she amazes students with details she's gleaned about them from their supervisors, such as, "Mary, your cat thinks very highly of you." Used midsession, the cookies contain humorous motivating messages, such as, "Mike, the registration form will become like a brother to you." As a closer, Garner uses the fortunes as a chance to recognize participants' efforts. A sample message may read, "Joan, your hard work will come back to you tenfold."

Garner uses name tents to ensure she distributes the cookies to their rightful owners.

86

Customized fortune cookies motivate trainees

87

Pasta 'prizes' increase recall, motivation

A dollar's worth of spaghetti and a box of giveaway goodies can go a long way toward reinforcing desired performance. Michelle Deck and Jeanne Silva of Ochsner Hospital in Metairie, LA, use pasta "prizes" as a motivation tool and reinforcer in their training sessions.

Participants can earn pieces of pasta as rewards by:
- Arriving on time.
- Returning from breaks on time.
- Giving correct individual responses to questions.
- Giving correct small group responses to questions.

At two intervals in the program they conduct "pasta auctions." Participants with pasta awards use them to buy prizes — promotional items the hospital receives free, including pens, flashlights, cups, visors, watches, and clipboards.

Deck and Silva say participants arrive early for programs, return promptly from breaks, encourage colleagues attending future programs to arrive early, choose more challenging questions to answer to win larger amounts of pasta, share pasta so other small group members can buy prizes, and have a good laugh about the fact they are involved in cutthroat competition over bits of macaroni.

Cartoons or magazine illustrations can be enlarged to provide inexpensive, thought-provoking posters for the training classroom. Sherrie Spilde, training specialist with the state of South Dakota personnel bureau, has a simple technique.

She makes a photocopy of the art on an overhead transparency, projects it on a flip chart or poster board, and traces the enlarged image with markers. The images are easily stored or transported in cardboard tubes.

88

Poster-size cartoons provoke thought

89

Apples provide metaphor about expectations

A Confucius-like look at a piece of fruit makes a valuable point in Dr. Beverly Smallwood and Kate Andrews' management development sessions.

Smallwood and Andrews, organizational consultants with Smallwood Associates in San Diego, CA, supply pairs of trainees with a plastic knife and an apple. They then instruct them to cut their apples in half and count the seeds. Next, they ask participants to count the apples in one seed — an impossible task.

Smallwood and Andrews use this idea — that there is the "promise" of apples in the seed, if it can be planted and nurtured— to discuss how the ideas, programs, policies, and projects that management trainees plant as leaders take time to develop. Their discussions usually focus on the point that impatience and unrealistic expectations deliver few results, except disappointment.

Stella Spalt, manager of management development for the American Red Cross in St. Louis, MO, puts some pop into her review sessions by challenging participants to burst balloons and then answer the questions written on slips of paper inside.

This can be done individually or with teams, with prizes provided for correct answers. A variation is to use balloon color to signify question difficulty and the number of points awarded. For instance, red balloons might be worth five points, blue balloons 10 points, and so on.

90

Balloons put some pop into review sessions

91

Intercom provides inexpensive, two-way interaction

To help train new employees how to manage phone calls with customers, trainer Herbert Luxton of Minidata purchased a $50 intercom system.

The intercom system uses existing electrical lines and requires virtually no installation. Luxton is able to "call" each of the trainees from another room with a typical customer situation. A second instructor sets the stage for the call and coordinates the information the trainee has available for problem-solving.

The intercom lets the entire training class monitor the conversation and participate in problem-solving. The trainee using the phone is instructed to use fellow trainees as the first resource in the problem-solving steps, keeping the entire group involved and alert.

During a train-the-trainer presentation for the Florida Department of Highway Safety and Motor Vehicles, trainer Rene Starnes emphasizes that trainers mold, shape, and design the work-force of tomorrow with the quality training programs they present today.

First Starnes discusses some of the intangible qualities that transform a mediocre trainer into an excellent trainer. She lists the qualities on a flip chart. Participants are then asked to choose the quality from that list which they would most like to have. At this point, Starnes passes out Play-Doh and asks that they turn that important intangible quality into a tangible product, a sculpture that would represent quality.

Starnes says the group is initially skeptical, but has fun once they begin molding the sculptures. Each participant exhibits his or her creation and explains its meaning.

For example, one participant made a flower pot with buds poking up and related it to training by saying the flowers were program participants who would develop and grow from the nurturing and empathy of the trainer during the session.

92

Show trainees how to mold tomorrow's workforce

93

Remote control gives you mobility

Consider investing in a remote control device for your overhead projector to improve your mobility around a class. David Pomeroy, a technical trainer with gas fireplaces, bought a remote control for his projector so he can turn the overhead on or off from anywhere in the room when he wants to make a point, while strolling through the audience.

A collection of old hats used in leadership training helps illustrate the roles people play in groups and makes role-playing more fun, says Carol Webb, staff development specialist, Clemson University, Clemson, SC. Webb asks participants to pull a hat out of a bag, then gives them a role to play or read in front of the group. She says participants usually have fun with the exercise, especially if there are a variety of hats for props.

Webb says the technique can also be used for helping attendees understand different personality types or the readiness level of different employees in supervisory training.

94

Old hats illustrate roles people play in groups

95

Simple graphics provide instant assessment

Don Valencic, a trainer for Boeing Commercial Airplane, monitors class comprehension with this technique: He makes a paper puzzle, usually a circle divided into wedges, for each participant. A word or phrase that represents a concept to be presented during class is written on each piece.

As each student fully understands a concept, he or she tapes the appropriate wedge or puzzle piece on the wall. Valencic only needs to look around the room to see if puzzle pieces are missing to know whether a trainee needs more time or help on a particular concept. At the end of the session, all puzzles should be complete.

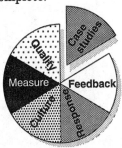

As each student understands a concept, he or she tapes the appropriate wedge on the wall. At the end of the session, all "pies" should be complete.

The phrase, "pass the buck," takes on a whole new meaning in review exercises conducted by LeeAnn Downey, corporate trainer for Guaranty National Insurance in Englewood, CO. In the exercise, participants must define a concept that was presented in class in order to pass the $10 or $20 bill along. If a participant cannot think of a concept not previously defined by someone else, he or she must pass the bill and is no longer in the game. The last person to correctly define a concept keeps the bill.

96

Money incentive encourages participation during reviews

97

Collage becomes collection of learning points

A collage created by trainees on a classroom wall that depicts major learning points acts as a review for students of Cathy Cady, manager of education for Southwestern Bell.

Cady randomly cuts out pictures from catalogs and magazines and brings them to class. (She also encourages students to bring cutouts from home.) Throughout a week-long class, she has students choose pictures to paste into the collage that reinforce lessons taught. As the collage grows it becomes a reminder of the major learning points. At the end of the class, Cady gives the completed collage to a student as a reward.

Looking for the final word on those pesky questions with answers that depend on the method of interpretation? Simply turn to the "magic 8-ball," says Connie Kelly, a senior training consultant at Continental Bank in Chicago. She introduces her magic 8-ball at the beginning of the program explaining that it will be the final answer on questions with more than one answer. The magic 8-ball is a toy made by Tyco that looks like an 8-ball, but is filled with liquid. Inside there's a many-sided dye with cryptic answers on each side. The dye floats to a small window at the bottom of the 8-ball when turned upside down.

When debate on a subject turns into an issue of interpretation in her credit accounting training course, Kelly says, "Let's ask the 8-ball." For example, Kelly might ask the 8-ball, "Does management understand the significance of the extra work this practice requires for our accountants? Answer: "The answer is unclear. Try again later."

She says, students typically accept the 8-ball's answer, and it allows Kelly to insert humor in situations that can be contentious.

98

Clairvoyant toy gets trainers out from behind the 8-ball

99

Mystery index cards serve as end-of-session review

Janine Sayles, an education specialist with the Center for Nursing Education, Greater Southeast Community Hospital, Washington, DC, uses this fast and easy technique to review course content at the end of a training day.

Sayles writes words or concepts she'll cover in class on colorful 3 x 5 inch index cards. As trainees return from lunch or as they arrive in the morning for half-day sessions, she greets them at the door and has each person pick an index card. She holds the cards face down.

At the end of class she explains the "mystery" of the cards. Whoever holds the card with the word or concept that completes a phrase or definition Sayles reads aloud — or writes on an overhead — should hold that card up and read it aloud. When participants give the correct response, Sayles throws them a small "goodie," which usually is anything from candy wrapped in colorful cloth and tied with ribbon to colorful Post-it note pads.

> At the beginning of a session, distribute 3x5 index cards that contain key words or phrases that "fill in the blanks" during a review session.

To illustrate that first impressions often lead to faulty conclusions, Anna Rouhana, a training coordinator at the University of Miami, Coral Gables, FL, uses this exercise in customer service training sessions.

After a brief discussion on communication styles and the impressions body language, tone, and choice of words make, Rouhana brings out plain brown bags and colorful presents. She then asks each participant to choose one, based on their first impressions. After they choose a box or bag, she asks those who chose the bag to dig in and pull out what's inside — usually a "warm fuzzy" gift of some sort. Those who choose the present find a penny (for their thoughts) inside.

She asks the group whether reality matched first perceptions — did they expect to find what they did? What were their initial choices based on? A discussion follows on image and appearance. "We all make assumptions based on appearances," Rouhana says, "but when we take the time to 'look inside' we often find much more or less than we expected."

100

Show trainees negative side of first impressions

Notices on students' paychecks heighten interest

Here's a marketing tip virtually guaranteed to boost attendance in your classes: Use your company's paycheck stubs to alert participants to upcoming classes. Nina Hollingsworth, training supervisor with Mead Coated Board in Phenix City, AL, does just that for trainees in a three-phase pre-supervisory training program.

Previously when Hollingsworth sent out reminders of upcoming training classes she spent a lot of time copying, folding, and attaching the announcements to time cards. Now, with the help of the staff that generates the paychecks, she says students can be reminded about courses with a minimum of time and hassle. The payroll staff simply enters a brief reminder of when the class is scheduled and prints it on each participant's paycheck stub.

About the Author...

Robert Pike has been developing and implementing training programs for business, industry, government, and other professions since 1969. As president of Creative Training Techniques International Inc., Resources for Organizations Inc., and The Resources Group Inc., he leads more than 150 sessions each year on topics such as leadership, attitudes, motivation, communication, decision-making, problem-solving, personal and organizational effectiveness, conflict management, team-building, and managerial productivity.

More than 50,000 trainers have attended Pike's Creative Training Techniques workshops. As a consultant, he has worked with such organizations as American Express, Upjohn, Hallmark Cards Inc., IBM, PSE&G, Bally's Casino Resort, and Shell Oil. A member of the American Society for Training and Development (ASTD) since 1972, he has served on three of the organization's national design groups, and held office as director of special interest groups and as a member of the national board.

An outstanding speaker, Pike has been a presenter at regional and national conferences for ASTD and other organizations. He currently serves as co-chairman of the Professional Emphasis Groups for the National Speakers' Association. He was recently granted the professional designation of Certified Speaking Professional (CSP) by the NSA, an endorsement earned by only 170 of the organization's 3,800 members.

Pike is editor of Lakewood Publications' *Creative Training Techniques Newsletter*, author of *The Creative Training Techniques Handbook*, and has contributed articles to *TRAINING Magazine*, *The Personnel Administrator*, and *Self-Development Journal*. He has been listed, since 1980, in *Who's Who in the Midwest* and is listed in *Who's Who in Finance and Industry*.

Want More Copies?

This and most other Lakewood books are available at special quantity discounts when purchased in bulk. For details write Lakewood Books, 50 South Ninth Street, Minneapolis, MN 55402. Call (800) 707-7769 or (612) 333-0471. Or fax (612) 340-4819. Visit our web page at www.lakewoodpub.com.

More on Training

Powerful Audiovisual Techniques: 101 Ideas to Increase the
   Impact and Effectiveness of Your Training $14.95

Dynamic Openers & Energizers: 101 Tips and Tactics for
   Enlivening Your Training Classroom $14.95

Optimizing Training Transfer: 101 Techniques for Improving
   Training Retention and Application $14.95

Managing the Front-End of Training: 101 Ways to Analyze
   Training Needs — And Get Results! $14.95

Motivating Your Trainees: 101 Proven Ways to Get Them
   to Really Want to Learn $14.95

Creative Training Techniques Handbook: Tips, Tactics, and
   How-To's for Delivering Effective Training, 2nd Ed. $49.95

Creative Training Techniques Newsletter: Tips, Tactics, and
   How-To's for Delivering Effective Training $ 99/12 issues